Easy Peasy English

Written by
Sue McMillan

Illustrated by
Dave Semple

Scholastic Children's Books
Euston House, 24 Eversholt Street
London NW1 1DB

A division of Scholastic Ltd
London ~ New York ~ Toronto ~ Sydney ~ Auckland
Mexico City ~ New Delhi ~ Hong Kong

Published in the UK by Scholastic Ltd, 2014

ISBN 978 1 407 14445 0

Printed and bound by Tien Wah Press Pte. Ltd, Singapore

2 4 6 8 10 9 7 5 3 1

Papers used by Scholastic Children's Books are made from
wood grown in sustainable forests.

Contents

Foreword

What would be the first thing you think of when you hear the word 'grammar'? If you're anything like my children, your eyes will glaze over and you'd be doing one of those mental yawns that you can't quite stifle, no matter how hard you try. In my job I spend a lot of time trying to show people that words really are some of the most exciting things in the world. And grammar simply gives us the tools to put them together. We all use it every day, instinctively - without it we wouldn't be able to communicate a thing! Why then does it get such a raw deal?

The answer probably lies in our past, and the images most of us still have of fusty teachers using dusty books to teach us crusty rules. But it doesn't have to be that way, and that's where *Easy-Peasy English* comes in − a grammar guide that gives you all the basics, but without the boring bits.

Here at last is a book that you can dip in and out of to get the lowdown on everything from parts of speech, tenses and punctuation to spelling and spicing up your writing. The book is perfectly aimed at children in years 5 and 6; it will help them get to grips with the curriculum and prepare them for secondary school. But it's not all about school. The book is full of tips for great writing in real life, from thank-you letters and emails to stories and creative writing.

How I wish I'd had this book when I was growing up. At least I can give it to my own kids. And if I ever dare mention the word 'grammar', I can't wait for them to reply, "Mum, it's *Easy Peasy*"!

Susie Dent

Chapter 1

Let's Go!

Sometimes you may feel as though knowing how to speak and write properly doesn't matter. Maybe you think it's old-fashioned or uncool, but I bet if you sit back and think about it you'll realize that the way you speak and act with your mates is probably not the way you are around your gran or your teachers.

If you like, imagine that there are two of you. There's the person you are when you're chatting with your friends – relaxed and informal. But there's also the more formal person you need to be around elderly relatives and in school tests. This is why knowing how to use language is important, because you never know when your more formal side will be needed.

So, if you think this book is going to force you to speak and write like someone from Victorian times, you're wrong! What it will teach you is the basics without the boring bits. It will give you the skills you need so that, whatever the situation (whether it's writing a thank-you letter or taking an English test), you'll know just what to say or write, and do it with confidence.

If it helps, think of language as a toolbox. If you've never used tools before, when you first look in the box, there is a baffling collection of bits and pieces that look really complicated. Grab a random tool and your task will go a bit pear-shaped. It's much better to find out what each one is for and how to use it. The same is true of English – if you know what everything is for and how to use it, it's easy peasy! So let's open up the language toolbox and find out what all those mysterious bit and pieces are for...

What to Use and When

We all know that it's fine to be casual with your mates, but there are times when you need to be more formal when you write or speak to someone.

Chances are that you already know how to deal with some situations. It's a no-brainer that when you are chilling out with your friends you can use slang, in-jokes and text-talk.

On the other hand, if you are meeting the Queen then a fist-bump and shouting, 'Alright, Liz?' is likely to land you in a whole lot of trouble at Buckingham Palace and that's before you consider that your parents will probably make sure that you're grounded for the rest of your life.

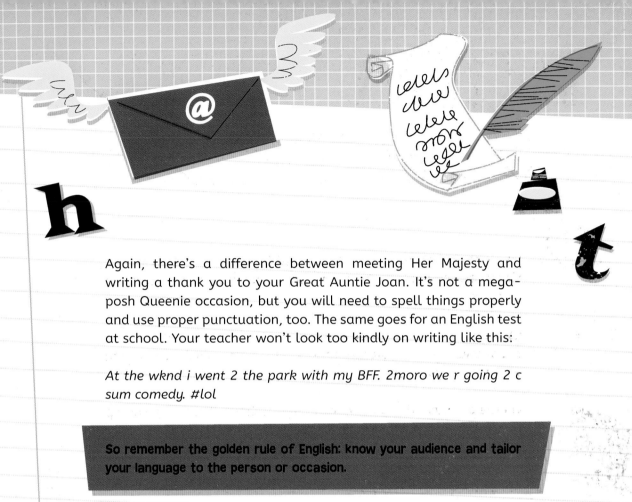

Again, there's a difference between meeting Her Majesty and writing a thank you to your Great Auntie Joan. It's not a mega-posh Queenie occasion, but you will need to spell things properly and use proper punctuation, too. The same goes for an English test at school. Your teacher won't look too kindly on writing like this:

At the wknd i went 2 the park with my BFF. 2moro we r going 2 c sum comedy. #lol

So remember the golden rule of English: know your audience and tailor your language to the person or occasion.

Who Needs , Rules?

Did you know that there are so many words in the English language that even the experts cannot agree on how many there are? With thousands to choose from, it's no wonder that we need some rules.

Imagine if we all slapped words down on the page in any order and without any punctuation to show where our thoughts stop, start and change. It would be pretty messy. Now imagine that every person in the world had their own version of language, so what one person called 'a car' someone else called 'a tree' and so on. There would be no way of communicating at all.

Thankfully, we have a rule that says we all use the same words for the same things. That way, we all know that 'a car' is a particular kind of motorized vehicle. 'A red car' is a vehicle of that colour. 'Dad's red car' means the vehicle of that colour that belongs to your father.

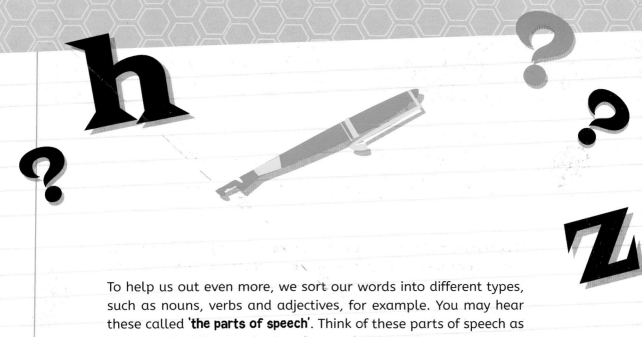

To help us out even more, we sort our words into different types, such as nouns, verbs and adjectives, for example. You may hear these called **'the parts of speech'**. Think of these parts of speech as being the building blocks that fit together to make a sentence. By learning how best to put the blocks together, and using punctuation and tenses to add even more meaning, our communication can be crystal clear.

This part of the book will teach you what each of these blocks is for and will help you start to build brilliant sentences.

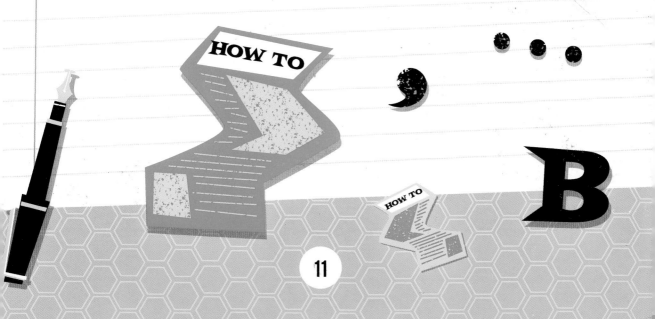

HOW TO

HOW TO

B

The Name Game

The first and most important rule of building sentences is knowing what we are talking about and to do this we need to give labels or names to objects, people and places.

Imagine the confusion if there were no names for things:
"I saw a doo-dah the other day. It ran out of the thingy."

It would be pretty confusing. It's so much easier to say:
"I saw a dog the other day. It ran out of the house."

Words that name things are called **'nouns'**. You can remember this easily because both nouns and names begin with 'n'.

When you use words like *'dog'* and *'house'* you are using **common nouns**. These are words that you can put *'the'*, *'a'* or *'an'* in front of. *'Car'*, *'horse'*, *'bike'*, *'book'* and *'table'* are examples of common nouns.

Perfectly proper

If you want to tell your friend about a particular person or thing, you use a **'proper noun'**:

"I saw Sarah Jones the other day. She ran out of Euston Station."

'Sarah Jones' and *'Euston Station'* are the names of a particular person and place. Did you notice that they start with a capital letter? That's a good way to spot a proper noun, as they all do.

Here's a sentence that uses both common and proper nouns:
"Of my <u>friends</u>, <u>Ben</u> is the silliest."

organizing Groups

When you want to talk about a group of people or things, you can use a **'collective noun'**.

If your teacher says things like, *"Right class, let's get started,"* she is using the collective noun *'class'* so you know that she is talking to all of you.

This is a lot easier than her saying, *"Right, Robbie, Fatima, Hannah, Jake, Logan, Amelia, Abdul..."* which would take most of the lesson!

Other collective nouns you may have heard include *'an army'* (of soldiers), *'a library'* (of books) and *'a choir'* (of singers).

Did You Know?

There are some great collective nouns for animals, such as 'a murder' of crows, 'a smack' of jellyfish and 'a pandemonium' of parrots.

13

Me, Myself and I

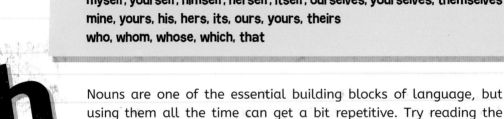

Nouns are one of the essential building blocks of language, but using them all the time can get a bit repetitive. Try reading the passage below out loud, and see for yourself:

Bob was walking down the street when a lion appeared from nowhere. Roaring, the lion chased Bob down the street. The lion's hot breath was on Bob's neck. Bob was very scared of the lion. Could Bob outrun the lion or would the lion eat Bob? The lion got closer. The lion's snapping jaws were so close now...

Are you asleep yet? It gets a bit dull with all the **'Bobs'** and **'lions'** doesn't it? Luckily, we can spice things up by swapping some of the nouns and replacing them with **'pronouns'**:

Bob was walking down the street when a lion appeared from nowhere. Roaring, it chased him down the street. Its hot breath was on Bob's neck. He was very scared. Could he outrun it or would it eat him? The lion got closer. Its snapping jaws were so close now...

In this example the nouns are **'Bob'** and **'lion'**. **'Bob'** was swapped for **'he'** and **'him'** in places. **'Lion'** was swapped for **'it'**.

I, **you**, **he**, **she**, **it**, **we** and **they** are all pronouns - use these pronouns in sentences where the person or thing is doing the action. If the person or thing is having the action done to it, you would use: **me**, **you**, **him**, **her**, **it**, **us** or **them**. For example: *"I gave the book to her."*

Relatively easy

Some pronouns can be used to join different parts of a sentence and explain their relationship. These are known as '**relative pronouns**'. For example:

*"This is the cat **that** scratched my hand!"*
*"My friend **who** saw the band play live said they were terrible!"*
*"My new jeans are purple, **which** is my favourite colour."*

Quick Tip:

Take care using pronouns. It's easy to change the meaning of a sentence if you use them incorrectly. Look at these examples, which show how the meaning can change...

'Mum looked after her.' Here, Mum is caring for someone else. versus...
'Mum looked after herself.' Here, Mum is only thinking about what she wants – maybe a nice hot bubble bath and a good book!

You also need to make sure that it's clear who you are talking about when you use more than one pronoun in a sentence:

Dave drove Jim to work and he thought his driving was fantastic!

Who thinks Dave is a good driver? Dave or Jim?

Action!

They say that actions speak louder than words, but without action words, you can't make a sentence. The tools you need to describe the actions of people or things are also known as 'doing words' or 'verbs'.

*Tom **plays** guitar. Ruby **reads** a book. Ben **eats** potatoes.*

English has hundreds of verbs to choose from – far too many to be listed here. You can look up more verbs online or in a dictionary.

The trouble with using simple sentences like the examples above is that it does not give people much information. It doesn't tell people when something is happening, or if it is something that is going to happen in the future. Imagine you ask your mum for a lift somewhere and she says: *"I work."*

This tells you that your mum has a job. It doesn't give enough information for you to know that it is why she cannot give you a lift. What you need is more information to make the sentence totally clear. So, if your Mum tells you: *"I am working."* You know that she is busy doing her job right now and she can't give you a lift. In the example above, adding **'am'** – from the verb **'to be'** – tells you that something is happening right now. 'Am' is what's called a **'helping verb'**. You might hear your teacher call them **'auxiliary verbs'** instead.

Helping verbs are important because without them some sentences don't make sense at all. Another helping verb that you probably use all the time is **'to do'**. It is really useful for asking questions:

"Do you like hot chocolate?"

It can also stand in for the main verb when you answer a question: "*Yes, I do.*" (Instead of having to repeat: "*Yes, I like hot chocolate.*")

It can form negatives: "*I do not want to go to Jake's party.*"

It can also add emphasis: "*Oh, do come to the party. I know you'll enjoy it!*"

Some helping verbs, such as **can/could**, **may/might**, **will/would**, **shall/should** can also change the meaning of a sentence. So, for example:

"*I will come to the party*" means something different to:
"*I might come to the party.*"

Another useful helping verb is '**to have**':
I have seen the band play live.
She has parachuted from a plane.

I'm sure you use the helping verb '**to be**' all the time without realizing:

I am eating my breakfast.
He is cycling to school.
They are going to walk to school.

In the above examples, our helping verbs, plus the right verb endings help us to explain clearly to people when the action takes place. This is known as the '**tense**'. To find out how to make sense of tenses, turn to page 32. You can also find a complete list of helping verbs on page 94.

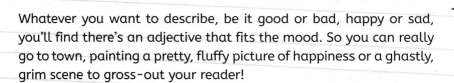

Adjectives

Sometimes, when you are talking or writing about something or someone, you need to be able to give more detail so people can picture it in their heads. 'Describing words', or 'adjectives', can help you to create a vivid picture for a reader or listener.

Whatever you want to describe, be it good or bad, happy or sad, you'll find there's an adjective that fits the mood. So you can really go to town, painting a pretty, fluffy picture of happiness or a ghastly, grim scene to gross-out your reader!

Wonderful words

Adjectives can describe things that make us feel all warm and fuzzy. You might say something is 'beautiful', 'amazing' or 'gorgeous'. For example:

*The meal we had last night was **amazing**. The lamb was **beautiful** and the dessert was **gorgeous**!*

Disgusting detail

They can also be used to create a really gross image:

*The hotel room was **disgusting**. The bathroom was **filthy**. The carpet was really **nasty**!*

Absolutely anything

Anything and everything can be described by using an adjective.

Use them on people...
*His smile is so **dazzling**.*
*She had a really **awful** haircut.*

Places and things...
*The elephant was **enormous**.*
*Molly's mum has a **blue** car.*

And even how you feel...
*I'm **grumpy** in the mornings.*
*Lizzie was so **excited** about the party.*

Better or best?

You can also use adjectives to compare things or tell someone which is the best, or worst.

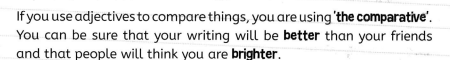

If you use adjectives to compare things, you are using **'the comparative'**. You can be sure that your writing will be **better** than your friends and that people will think you are **brighter**.

Adjectives can also be used to tell people which is the best or worst. This is known as **'the superlative'**. If you master these, people may start to say that you are the **best** in the class, or the **most likely** to succeed in English.

Quick tip:

If you are struggling to recall what an adjective is, remember: Adjectives **'add'** something to the noun.

Adverbs

So now you know about people and objects, and how to describe them. But what do you use when you want to talk about how something happens, or when it takes place, or how often?

For this, you need **'adverbs'**. As their name suggests, these are words that 'add' more description to a verb.

Often adverbs are made by adding '-ly' on the end of an adjective. Here are some examples.

How?

These adverbs tell you **how** something is being done:

*He eats **loudly**.*
*The dog creeps **quietly**.*
*The dog **quickly** stole the food.*

When?

These adverbs talk about **when** something is done:

*"I **often** play football."*
*"**Yesterday**, I broke my ankle."*
*"My ankle needs to heal **before** I play again."*
*"**Today** I am having the plaster removed."*

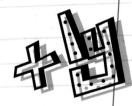

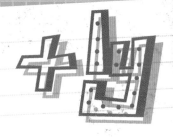

Where?

Adverbs can also be used to show **where** something happens:

*He searched **outside**.*
*"Have you looked **there**?"*
*His keys were **nowhere** to be seen.*

To what extent?

Some adverbs can be used to show **to what extent** something is happening. These might sound trickier, but actually they are sure to be words you use all the time, without even realizing it. For example:

*He had **almost** finished his homework.*
*It was **quite** windy.*
*She had **hardly** touched her lunch.*

Quick tip:
Most 'how' adverbs end in '-ly'.

Positions, Please!

Imagine you are trying to tell someone where you left your book. You will need to describe to them where it is in relation to other things:

"I left my book in the living room on the table."

To do this, you use **'prepositions'** such as **'in'** and **'on'**. It might seem like a tricky word but you can remember it easily, because prepositions contain 'positions'.

Here are some other examples of prepositions:

*He drove the car **on** the road that ran **between** the mountains.*

*She leaned **against** the wall.*

*The school is **near** the library.*

When?

Prepositions can also tell people when things happen in relation to each other:

*She was born **in** 2004.*

*She stayed at the birthday party **until** the cake was cut.*

*The prizes were given out **after** the game.*

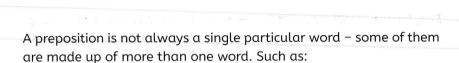

A preposition is not always a single particular word – some of them are made up of more than one word. Such as:

The horse trotted **out of** the stable.

Their meal was ruined **because of** the poor service.

The wasp was **on top of** the birthday cake.

The smoke was blown **away from** the houses.

Here are some of the most common prepositions:

above	during	opposite
after	for	outside
at	in/into	over
before	inside	to
behind	like	towards
beneath	near	under
beside	of	until
between	off	with
by	on/onto	

Get Connected

Now you know what some of the tools in your English toolbox are for, we can begin to look at building sentences. Take this simple sentence:

"My mum was really cross. Her car had a flat tyre. She had to walk to the bank. She caught the bus home."

It's a bit stilted, so let's use some words to join things together:

"My mum was really cross because her car had a flat tyre. As a result, she had to walk to the bank and catch the bus home."

Joining words, or **'connectives'**, join a simple phrase (or clause, see page 36) to another, or link ideas in separate sentences. You can remember what they are by picturing them **connect**ing words together. In the sentences above, the connectives are **'because'**, **'as a result'** and **'and'**. Other examples include **'however'**, **'meanwhile'**, **'yet'** and **'also'**.

Sometimes, you may hear people talk about **'conjunctions'** instead of 'connectives'. Use the phrases with care – all conjunctions are connectives, but not all connectives are conjunctions! It's easy to remember which is which, because conjunctions always work within one sentence to join two parts together. Examples of conjunctions include: **'and'**, **'or'**, **'but'** and **'so'**:

*"I walked the dog **and** I fed the cat."*
*"He went to the park **but** it was closed."*
*"He broke his leg **so** he couldn't ski."*

Different types of conjunctions link different things. Conjunctions that join two parts of a sentence that are equally important are called **'coordinating conjunctions'**. Think of them as two parts of an outfit – a top and a pair of trousers. Examples of coordinating conjunctions include **'and'**, **'but'**, **'or'**, **'yet'** and **'so'**.

*"I like pizza **but** pasta is my favourite."*

Some conjunctions gives readers extra information that isn't as important as the other rest of the sentence. These are called **'subordinate conjunctions'** and include words such as **'although'**, **'because'**, **'since'** and **'as'**.

*"I overslept **although** I set my alarm."*

To compare things you need a **'correlative conjunction'** – correlative means relating to each other. They come in pairs, so you may see: **'either/or'**, **'whether/or'** and **'neither/nor'**, for example:

*"She's **neither** kind **nor** helpful."*

Then there are conjunctions that are made up of more than one word. These are called **'compound conjunctions'** and include: **'as long as'**, **'so that'** and **'as soon as'**.

*"I will do my homework **as soon as** I have beaten my high score."*

You'll find a full list of conjunctions and connectives on pages 94 and 95.

Chapter 2

F

S

Eloquent

Triumph

Piquant

Ambitious

Yearn

Impetus

Jocular

Ergo

Incogitable

Paragon

G

I

y'

A Way with Words

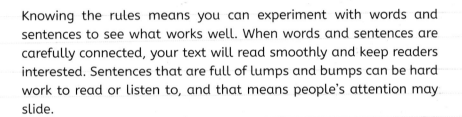

So now you know what the basic language building blocks are called, the next step is to find out how they fit together.

Learning to be a slick speaker or a wonderful writer is about more than just putting the words in the right order on the page. It is also about picking your words carefully so that the reader knows exactly what you mean.

Knowing the rules means you can experiment with words and sentences to see what works well. When words and sentences are carefully connected, your text will read smoothly and keep readers interested. Sentences that are full of lumps and bumps can be hard work to read or listen to, and that means people's attention may slide.

The easiest way to find any sticking points or lumpy words in a piece of text is to read it aloud. Then you can start to smooth them out. The more you practise, the easier it gets and before you know it, you'll have perfectly polished prose at your fingertips!

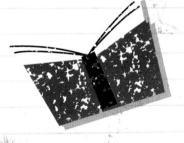

Know Your Subjects From Your Objects

The simplest sentences of all contain just two things: a noun and a verb. For example:

Sheep eat.

Boys play.

Girls dance.

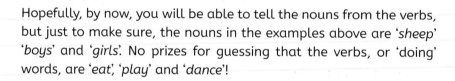

Hopefully, by now, you will be able to tell the nouns from the verbs, but just to make sure, the nouns in the examples above are '*sheep*' '*boys*' and '*girls*'. No prizes for guessing that the verbs, or 'doing' words, are '*eat*', '*play*' and '*dance*'!

Sometimes, you might hear people talk about **'the subject'** of a sentence. What they mean is whoever or whatever is doing the action.

In the examples above the subjects are the sheep that are eating, the boys who are playing and the girls who are dancing.

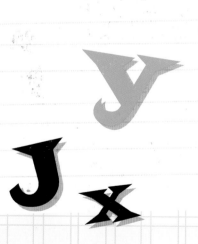

Here are some more examples to help you:

Sophie bounces.

Youssef shouts.

Dave cooks.

The subjects of these sentences are 'Sophie', 'Youssef' and 'Dave', because they are doing the actions.

Things get a little more complicated when objects get involved. Turn the page to find out more...

Did You Know?

A clause is a group of words that includes a subject and a verb. Some sentences have one clause, others may have several. Clauses can be equally important or one may be more important than the other. For example: *the girl, who had studied hard, passed her test.*

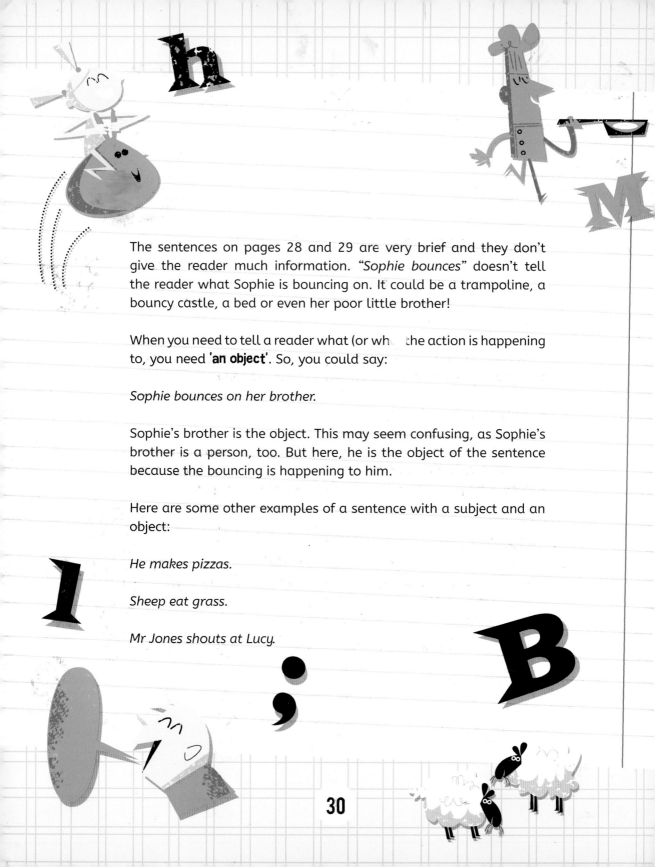

The sentences on pages 28 and 29 are very brief and they don't give the reader much information. "*Sophie bounces*" doesn't tell the reader what Sophie is bouncing on. It could be a trampoline, a bouncy castle, a bed or even her poor little brother!

When you need to tell a reader what (or wh the action is happening to, you need **'an object'**. So, you could say:

Sophie bounces on her brother.

Sophie's brother is the object. This may seem confusing, as Sophie's brother is a person, too. But here, he is the object of the sentence because the bouncing is happening to him.

Here are some other examples of a sentence with a subject and an object:

He makes pizzas.

Sheep eat grass.

Mr Jones shouts at Lucy.

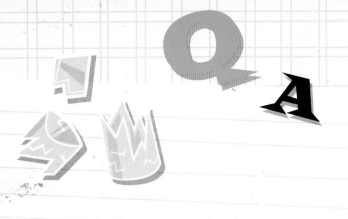
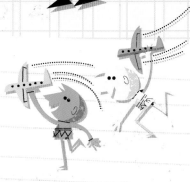

Active or passive?

If the subject is doing the action, the sentence is in what's called the **'active voice'**. Here's an example:

Jo smashed the glass.

If the action is being done TO the subject noun, you may see sentences that are written in what's known as the **'passive voice'**:

The glass was smashed by Jo.

Although the same thing has happened (a glass has been broken), in the first example, Jo (the subject) is doing the smashing. In the second example, the smashing is being done TO the glass.

Top Tip:

If you want to become a master at spotting passive sentences, a good place to look is on signs. They are often written in the passive voice. 'Dogs must be kept on a lead' is a good example. See how many you can spot when you're out and about.

31

Tense Sense

Being able to tell someone when something happened is really useful. In many languages, including English, we have a handy way of flagging up if something has already happened, is happening right now, or will happen in the future. It's a bit like having a language time machine. The proper name for this is 'tenses' - here's how to make sense of them...

All in the past

When you want to tell someone about something that happened in the past, you use the **'past tense'**. Most of the time, you can show this by adding '-ed' to the verb:

*I **played** football.*
*She **baked** cupcakes.*
*We **climbed** the mountain.*

Present and correct

If you want to tell someone about something that happens regularly, or is a fact, you use the **'present tense'**:

*I **play** football.*
*She **bakes** cupcakes.*
*We **climb** mountains.*

Live action!

Sometimes, you need to give more detail. If something is happening right this minute, and will continue to do so, you need to use what's known as the **'present continuous tense'**. This is where your helping verbs come in (see page 16)! So imagine that your mum is nagging you to clean the house. You might say: *"I am doing my homework"*. By adding *'am'* (a 'to be' helping verb), she will know that you are working right this minute. Unless she checks of course, and finds that really you are busy playing a game on your phone... then you will need to use another helping verb when you say *"I am sorry"*!

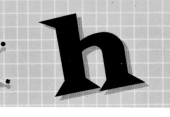

In the future

When you are talking about something that will happen in the future, you use the **'future tense'**:

*I **will play** football.*
*I **will bake** cupcakes.*
*We **will climb** the mountain.*

Did you notice that 'will' has been added to the examples? This tells someone that you are planning to do something, or have agreed that you will do something.

If you are planning to do something, but don't have a definite time in mind, you say 'going to' instead of 'will'. So you might say:

*I am **going to** bake cupcakes.*
*I am **going to** fly to the moon.*

Tricky tenses

For most verbs you can follow the rules above. But there are a few rule-breakers that don't follow the pattern. The proper word for them is **'irregular verbs'**.

Probably the best known irregular verb is 'go'. If we are talking in the past tense, we don't say:

"I goed to the cinema". Instead we say *"I went".*

Another example is 'drink'. We don't say *"I drinked the water"*, we say, *"I drank the water"*. With irregular verbs, it's just a case of learning them. You probably know most of them by now, but if not, you can find a list of irregular verbs on page 91. Alternatively, there are plenty of irregular verb lists online to help you.

All Agreed

When you are making sentences, it's important to make sure that the subject and verb agree. But this type of agreement isn't about getting along and having the same opinions.

Agreement in language is about making sure that you don't use the wrong ending for your verb. As a guide, most verbs stay the same if you are talking about 'I', 'you', 'we' or 'they' doing something and change if you use 'he', 'she' or 'it'.

Take this example:

I play.
You play.
We play.
They play.

He plays.
She plays.
It plays.

If you are ever unsure, remember that the subject of a sentence (the one doing the action) is what decides which verb ending you should use. Sometimes, you may find that the subject and the verb are not next to each other in a sentence. This doesn't matter. You should still pick the verb ending that agrees with your subject. For example:

The plants on my desk belong to my mother.

Here the subject of the sentence, 'plants', is plural, so the verb, 'belong', is plural, too.

Here is another example to help you:

The dog from next door always growls at me.

In this sentence the subject, 'dog', is singular, so the verb, 'growls', is singular, too.

Getting Complex

You've probably realized by now that most of the time, when we speak or write, we use quite lengthy sentences. On their own, short pieces of information, which are known as 'phrases', don't tell us much. An example of a phrase would be 'the huge monster'.

Adding a verb transforms our phrase into a **'clause'** – sounds scary doesn't it? Well it's not. A clause is part of a sentence with a subject and a verb, such as: *'The huge monster roared'*. Top tip – you can remember this is a clause if you think of the monster's 'claws'!

In some sentences, such as this example, you will see a main clause – the important bit – and then another, less important, clause. This is known as a **'subordinate clause'**, because it isn't so important. You can recognize subordinate clauses, because on their own they don't make sense. Subordinate clauses often start with connectives such as *'while'*, *'because'* and *'until'*:

'The huge monster roared until they retreated.'

So by joining clauses and subordinate clauses we can make complex sentences. Complex sentences use adjectives, adverbs and prepositions to give readers information on the detail as well as how, when or where the action took place.

Now here's a challenge for you. How many clauses and subordinate clauses and parts of speech can you spot in this paragraph?

They cycle along the winding lane and whizz down the steep hill in the brilliant sunshine. Mia whoops as she lifts her feet from the pedals and freewheels around the corner. Then a clatter fills the air. Ben rushes over to find Mia in a tangled heap on the verge. "The pothole buckled my wheel!", Mia wails.

Plurals

English also has a cunning way of communicating the amount or number of things you are talking about. By changing the ending of a word, a reader will know if you are talking about one or many things or people. For example, if you mention 'the book' then people will know you are talking about one book rather than loads. The proper term for this is 'the singular'. By adding 's' to the end so it becomes 'the books', people know you are talking about more than one, also known as 'the plural'.

It's easy to make lots of singular nouns into plurals: *dog/dogs, cat/cats, car/cars*. Seems simple, doesn't it? Unfortunately, not all words can be made plural by adding 's'. Here's how to deal with pesky plurals:

Slippery sounds

If a word ends in '**ch**', '**sh**', '**s**', '**x**' and '**z**', or it has a '**sss**' sound at the end, add '**-es**' instead:

'Match' becomes *'matches'*, *'lash'* becomes *'lashes'*, *'glass'* becomes *'glasses'*, *'fix'* becomes *'fixes'*, *'fizz'* becomes *'fizzes'*.

'Y' is it different?

If a word ends in '**y**', how you make it plural depends on the letter that comes before the '**y**'.

If the word before is a vowel, you just add an '**s**':
'Day' becomes *'days'* and *'toy'* becomes *'toys'*.

If the word before the '**y**' is a consonant, take off the '**y**' and add '**-ies**':
'Cry' becomes *'cries'*, *'dry'* becomes *'dries'*, *'puppy'* becomes *'puppies'*.

oh dear!

Don't get overwhelmed by '**o**' endings. Some plurals need '**s**' – *'jumbo'* and *'piano'* become *'jumbos'* and *'pianos'*, for instance.

As a rule, most words where the letter before the **'o'** is a consonant are made plural by adding **'s'**.

Others need **'-es'** on the end: *'potatoes'*, *'tomatoes'*, *'heroes'* and *'torpedoes'*. These you'll just have to learn. Sorry!

Loafs or loaves?
Some words ending in **'f'** just need an **'s'**:

'Roof' becomes *'roofs'*, *'surf'* becomes *'surfs'* and *'cliff'* becomes *'cliffs'*.

Some words ending in **'f'** or **'-fe'** need the **'f'** or **'-fe'** taken off and **'-ves'** adding for a plural:

So, *'life'* becomes *'lives'*, *'leaf'* becomes *'leaves'*, *'wife'* becomes *'wives'* and *'shelf'* becomes *'shelves'*. But beware! There are many exceptions - for example, *'giraffe'* becomes *'giraffes'* – which means it's another case of learning the plurals as you go...

No change
Some stubborn words, such as: *aircraft, fish, sheep, deer, tuna* and *moose*, don't like change at all and stay the same whether they are singular or plural.

Weird ones
Guess what? Just to make life difficult, there are a few rebel words that just don't obey the rules: *'man'* becomes *'men'*, *'woman'* becomes *'women'* and *'foot'* becomes *'feet'*.

Kids do their own thing: *'child'* becomes *'children'*. Just like the irregular verbs you met on page 33, you just have to learn these rebel plurals.

Chapter 3

Mysterious Marks

What is the point of punctuation? Is your teacher a full-stop fiend, or comma crazy? Does it really matter that much? Well, yes, it does. Take this famous example - a professor decided to ask his class how they would punctuate a sentence. He wrote:

Woman without her man is nothing

So how would you add punctuation? The professor found that most men punctuated it like this:

Woman, without her man, is nothing.

They added punctuation to make the sentence read that without a man, a woman is nothing. On the other hand, most girls added punctuation like this:

Woman: without her, man is nothing.

This flips the meaning on its head entirely to mean that without a woman, a man is nothing!

Punctuation adds meaning to your writing, just as road signs and maps help you to make sense of a car journey. Have you ever noticed, though, that sometimes there are too many signs on the road? If a road is too busy or there is too much information, the driver's brain feels overwhelmed and they may miss something important. It's just the same with punctuation. Used correctly it will help readers to make sense of your words. Scatter punctuation marks about randomly and your poor reader might get lost! Read on to make sure you put your readers on the right road.

Knowing Where to Stop

One of the first punctuation marks that you learn about in school is the full stop. That little dot at the end of the sentence may look unimportant, but it tells readers a lot. As its name suggests, it usually tells readers to 'stop' for a moment. Full stops are used to separate sentences or statements - think of them as being a little like the stop signs on a road that tell drivers to slow down and pause for a moment before they continue driving.

Finish with a stop

All sentences start with a capital letter and finish with a full stop. As we discovered on page 28, the simplest sentences contain a subject and a verb, or maybe a subject, an object and a verb, but they all need a full stop to finish them off. For example:

Milly bakes cakes.

Julie paints pictures.

Full stops for short

Full stops can also be used to show if something is shortened, or **'abbreviated'**. One you will probably see a lot is *'e.g.'* which is short for the Latin term *'exempli gratia'* or *'for example'* to you and me. It's so much easier to write e.g. than to remember the tricky Latin words, isn't it?

Other examples you might see include:

- **v.** meaning '*versus*' for a match or competition: "*England v. Scotland*"
- **a.m.** or **p.m.** meaning '*ante meridiem*' (or '*before noon*') and '*post meridiem*' (or '*after noon*'): "*We're meeting at 10 a.m. tomorrow*".
- **i.e.** which is short for another Latin phrase: '*id est*' or '*in other words*': "*The party was in June, i.e. two months ago*".
- **A.S.A.P.** meaning '*as soon as possible*': "*Please reply A.S.A.P.*"

Quick tip:

If you want to be top of the class, avoid using '*e.g.*' when you've got your formal hat on. It is much better to write it out in full as '*for example*'.

Doctors don't stop!

Wait! Guess what? There's another one of those 'except for' rules coming, but if you crack this, you'll have full stops sorted.

Sometimes shortened versions of words don't have full stops after the letters. Probably the best example of this that many people get wrong is '*Dr*' – you may see it written as '*Dr.*' instead. This is called '**a contraction**'. It doesn't need a full stop because the last letter is there and only the middle letters of the word are missed out. The same is true of '*Mr*' and '*Mrs*'. You can learn this rule by remembering that 'Doctors DON'T STOP'.

"Let's Eat Grandma!"

Commas help sentences make sense. Using a comma can also totally change the meaning of a sentence. Take our example: "Let's eat Grandma!" At the moment, this is a call for you and your brothers and sisters to tuck in to your poor granny! Add a comma in and suddenly your sentence means something completely different. Now, instead of eating your grandmother, you are telling her it's time for lunch:

"Let's eat, Grandma!"

Take care with commas

So, you know they're important (and sometimes lifesaving for grandmas), but how do you use them? The answer is with care! Scattering commas madly through your sentences to try to impress people won't help at all. Here are some simple rules to help you know when to use them and when to leave them out:

1. Lists

Commas separate things in a list of three items or more.

I bought chocolate, eggs, beans and bacon.

Leave out the commas and all your food could be made of chocolate:

I bought chocolate eggs beans and bacon.

Notice that you don't need a comma before the word *'and'* unless leaving it out makes the items confusing:

For tea I had eggs, beans, bacon and chocolate.

For this list, unless you genuinely ate bacon and chocolate together (yuck!) it would be better to write:

For tea I had eggs, beans, bacon, and chocolate.

These lists could be words or they could be groups of words – phrases. We talked phrases on page 36 if you need a quick reminder. So you might write:

At the weekend I listened to music, went to the skate park, watched a film, then Dad asked me to wash the car.

2. Joining

You can also use commas to separate phrases or clauses in long sentences. This helps to make the meaning of the sentence clearer.

Molly tried to get the last box of chocolates, but another shopper got to them first.

Dave had booked a table at the pizza place, as he had eaten there last week.

3. A little bit extra

Sometimes, commas are used to separate out information that adds something to the sentence but isn't vital to it:

Sally, who was top of the class, always handed her homework in on time.

So if the part of the sentence between the commas is taken out, the remaining sentence should still make sense and the general meaning should stay the same.

Sally always handed her homework in on time.

4. Speech

If you are writing speech and it comes after information about who is talking, you add a comma like this:

Anna smiled and said, "I've been to the shops".

If the speech comes first, you add a comma at the end of it, to show that the information afterwards relates to the speaker.

"I want to go to the shops," wailed Anna.

The only time you don't use a comma is if the speech is a question or exclamation:

"Do you want to go to the shops?" asked Anna.

"Come to the shops!" exclaimed Anna.

For more on writing speech, see page 55.

More Short Stops

As well as commas, there are other types of short stops that help sentences make sense: brackets ( ), dashes -, colons : and semicolons ;.

(Extra information)

If you want to give your reader extra information, you can keep it separate from the rest of the sentence by putting a pair of brackets around the words. This extra information inside the brackets can add more to a sentence. For example:

James burned all of the cakes.

In the above example, James could be baking cakes for the first time, which would explain why he burned them. Add some extra information in brackets and readers may be surprised to hear that he burned the cakes:

James (a baker) burned all of the cakes.

A dash of dashes (-)

Pairs of dashes can also be used around extra information in the same way as brackets or commas:

James – a baker – worked all morning to create the cakes.

Alternatively you might see a single dash in a sentence, to show readers that you are adding an extra thought:

James followed his recipe carefully, but he forgot one thing – to set the oven timer.

Handy with hyphens (-)

Dashes add extra information or form a pause, but hyphens, which are shorter than dashes, do something different. They link two words together to make a new word, called a **'compound word'**. The hyphen tells people that the words belong to each other.

Quick tip:

Not all compound words need a hyphen. You'll get extra teacher points if you remember that adverbs ending in '-*ly*' do not need a linking hyphen. So, for example, you would write: '*freshly baked bread*' NOT '*freshly-baked bread*'. Remember that if you are unsure if a word should be hyphenated, it's best to check by looking it up in a dictionary.

Hyphens are used where two words are used together to describe a noun: "*When you are lifting red-hot dishes, remember to wear oven gloves.*" "*I really hate hard-boiled eggs!*"

Hyphens also clarify meaning – *red-hot dishes* are dishes that are extremely hot. *Red hot dishes* might be hot dishes that happen to be red.

Warning!

Take care with hyphens as they can totally change the meaning of your sentence:

'*A man eating shark*' describes a man snacking on some tasty shark.

'*A man-eating shark*' describes a shark that eats people.

Cool with colons (:)

Colons are used to introduce a list of things.

For my summer holiday I packed: T-shirts, flip-flops, shorts, pyjamas and a hat.

Make sure that you have: locked the windows, turned off the lights and taken out the rubbish.

You might also see it used in a sentence before an explanation:

Tara had a tummy ache: she'd eaten 42 cakes.

Here, you'll notice that first part of the sentence, before the colon, makes sense on its own. The part afterwards explains the main idea of the sentence in more detail — in the example above it explains exactly why Tara has a tummy ache by showing us that she has eaten far too many cakes.

Colons can also be used before a list of main points, such as in this ad:

Come and relax at Beaches Hotel where you can enjoy:
- *Our fully heated swimming pool and steam room.*
- *The spacious, well-equipped gymnasium with instructors.*
- *Evening entertainment in our Beach Café.*
- *Free entry to G-Force theme park and Splash water park.*

Semicolons sorted (;)

Semicolons are used when we want to have a slightly longer pause than a comma, but not the complete stop of a full stop. If it helps, think of them as 'mega commas'.

Semicolons are really useful for punctuating a list of phrases, which are short pieces of information (turn back to page 36 for a recap on phrases, if you need a reminder). Look at this example:

When we stayed at Beaches Hotel, we swam in the pool; we went to the G-Force theme park, which was great; Dad went to the gym, but it was closed for repair; and we saw the band play every night in the Beach Café.

Did you notice that some of the phrases in the sentence contain commas? If we had used commas to separate our phrases instead, it would not have been as clear. By using our mega commas – semicolons – to separate each phrase, readers know exactly what happened and where.

Quick tip:

If you're getting in a knot with this semicolon and comma business, try reading the example above aloud. Add a very small pause whenever you hit a comma, and a slightly longer pause when you come across a semicolon. You'll see how the sentence makes much more sense.

Semicolons can also be used to join two sentences together:

Sophie bought shoes with her birthday money; Ruth saved hers.

These sentences are linked and talking about the same thing – in this case what two girls did with their birthday money – BUT the part after the semicolon does not explain the first part. They are both of equal importance.

Apostrophes

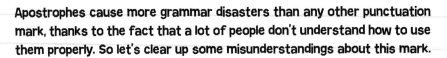

Apostrophes cause more grammar disasters than any other punctuation mark, thanks to the fact that a lot of people don't understand how to use them properly. So let's clear up some misunderstandings about this mark.

Missing letters

When two words are joined together and some letters have been missed out, we show this by using an apostrophe. Probably one of the best known ones is *'I'm'* which means *'I am'*. The words are joined and the *'a'* is missed out. The same is true of *'we are'*, which becomes *'we're'*, *'do not'*, which becomes *'don't'*, *'that is'*, which becomes *'that's'* and *'what is'*, which becomes *'what's'*.

Apostrophes can also be used when one word is shortened, such as when we shorten *'cannot'* to *'can't'*.

Does it belong?

Apostrophes are also used to show that something belongs to someone. To use it, we add apostrophe then an 's' to the owner:

Grace's book.

Here, the ''s' shows the reader that the book we are talking about belongs to Grace. We can also use it for things:

The book's pages.

If the word ends in 's' we still add 's' after the apostrophe (though it is also correct just to have an apostrophe after the final 's'):

Cerys's book. OR *Cerys' book.*

Group rules

If the thing in question belongs to a group of people or things, we simply add an apostrophe to the 's':

The girls' books.

But there are some exceptions. If the plural doesn't end in 's' we add ' 's', just as we do for one person or thing:

Children's books.
Men's toilets.
Women's changing rooms.

Pesky plurals

One of the biggest mistakes people make with apostrophes is adding one if something is plural. Remember, if it's not shortening two words, or it doesn't show belonging, then resist the urge to add the apostrophe.

It's tricky!

Many people also get confused by '*its*' and '*it's*'. So what's the difference? '*It's*' is a shortened version of '*it is*' or '*it has*':

"*It's scorching outside today!*"
"*It's been really boring at school today.*"

'*Its*' means '*belonging to it*':

"*Have you seen the polar bear? Its paws are enormous!*"

When you are writing '*its*' and aren't sure if you need an apostrophe, you can check by seeing if you can swap it for '*it is*'. If you can, you need an apostrophe. If you can't, leave it out!

"Really? Wow!"

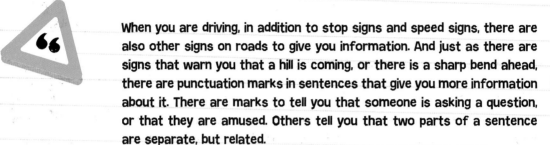

When you are driving, in addition to stop signs and speed signs, there are also other signs on roads to give you information. And just as there are signs that warn you that a hill is coming, or there is a sharp bend ahead, there are punctuation marks in sentences that give you more information about it. There are marks to tell you that someone is asking a question, or that they are amused. Others tell you that two parts of a sentence are separate, but related.

What is the question?

It's a no-brainer to guess that a question mark is used to show that a question is being asked:

Do you like my new shoes?
Did James burn the cakes again?
"Can you come for lunch?" asked Anna.

Always remember that unless your sentence asks a question, you don't need a question mark. So, if we were to change the last example round so it says: *"Anna asked if I could come for lunch."* We finish the sentence with a full stop.

Awesome!

When you are writing, how do you convey strong feelings to readers? Perhaps you want to show that someone was angry, surprised or ordering someone to do something? For these occasions, you need an exclamation mark:

Wait!
I was amazed!
Get lost!
I can't wait to see you!

Sometimes, people feel that adding extra exclamation marks really drives the point home. It doesn't, but it will drive your teacher mad!!!

She said what?

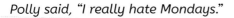

When you are writing, at some point you will need to show that someone is speaking. But it is important that these words are separated from the rest of the text, so that readers know where the speech starts and finishes. We add two little lines " " called '**inverted commas**', or speech marks, around the words someone says to set it apart from the rest of the sentence, like this:

Polly said, "I really hate Mondays."

The only time that you don't use speech marks is if you are telling people what someone has said in your own words. So you might say:

Polly said that she doesn't like Mondays.

Remember to put a comma before the first speech mark and add a full stop, comma, question mark or exclamation mark before the closing speech mark:

Emma said, "He's stolen my bag! Did anyone see which way he went?"

If the sentence is written the other way round, you still add a comma, question mark or exclamation mark before the closing speech mark:

"That's not fair! You promised we could go to the cinema!" cried Alfie.

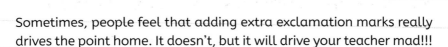
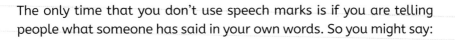

Chapter 4

Sparkling Spelling

Why do you get nagged about the way you spell words? As long as a word looks fairly recognizable, why can't we spell things how we want to? Is it really that important or is it just because your parents and teachers like to give you a hard time?

Take the word *'city'*, for example. If it was written as *'citie'* it would sound the same, wouldn't it? Way back in medieval times, spelling was such a free-for-all that there were around 500 ways to spell the word *'through'*. Yikes!

There's a whole history lesson on why words got so messy, but in a nutshell it all started because books were copied out by hand (can you imagine?!) or printed abroad. So it was pretty easy for the people producing the books to get in a bit of a spelling tangle. Why? Because they didn't speak the language! This is why so many mistakes slipped in. In fact, some books were so bad that words were spelled in several ways on the same page. How sloppy!

But the story doesn't end there. Early printers were paid by the line for their work. They soon realised that by adding an extra letter to a word here or there that they could stretch things out and earn some extra cash. How sneaky!

For a long time, people knew that spelling needed sorting. Teachers have been trying to fix scrambled spellings for centuries by choosing one way to spell a word and making lists for children to learn. So what does all this tell us? Two things. Number one: spelling things any old way has already been tried and it doesn't work. Number two: kids have probably been moaning about their spelling homework for hundreds of years...

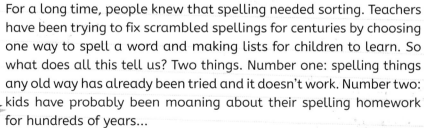

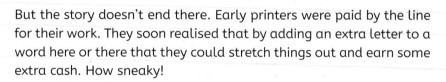

I before E...

Way back before all this spelling skullduggery started, 'friend' was spelled 'frend'. Wouldn't life be easier if it was still that way? Then you wouldn't have to worry about the pesky 'i' and 'e' and which comes first, which is a common cause of pain for many people.

Probably the easiest way to remember that 'i' comes before 'e' is to remember that in IDEA, 'i' is first. This only works for words that have a long 'ee' sound such as *believe* or *field*.

But guess what? There are still a few words that break this rule. *Seize* has a long 'ee' sound, but the 'e' comes first. So does *protein* and *caffeine*.

I 'see'

If the 'i' and 'e' come after 'c', then you swap them round. You may have heard people say "i before e except after c", but again, this only works for words with long 'ee' sounds such as *receive*, *piece* and *receipt*.

No 'ee', no 'c'

Some words don't follow the 'i before e' rule, because the sound the vowels make is not a long 'ee'. So remember that when words have an 'i' sound, such as in *height*, *neither* and *either* the 'e' comes before the 'i'.

The same is true for words that make an 'ay' sound, like *'neighbour'*, *'weigh'*, *'vein'* and *'eighty'*.

Shhh!

Words where the letter 'ci' make a 'shh' sound, break the 'except after c' part of the rule. This includes words such as *'ancient'*, *'conscience'* and *'efficient'*.

You also need to take care with the 'i before e' rule when you change the ending of the word, because word endings have their own rules that are more important. When you change *'fancy'* to *'fancied'*, the 'i' comes before the 'e', even though it is after 'c'. The same is true of words like *'emergency'*, which becomes *'emergencies'* and *'juicy'* which becomes *'juicier'* or *'juiciest'*. You can find out more about word endings on pages 36 and 61.

So what does all this tell us? That 'i before e, except after c' isn't much of a rule at all – it's more of a rough guide, because there are just as many words that break it as follow it. How weird! As always, if you're not sure, look it up in the dictionary.

Think about the word 'loyal' - it can be used to describe a friend who is reliable and always there for you. But imagine that this friend does something really nasty to you, like telling everyone at school your deepest darkest secret. Then you might say that they have been 'disloyal'. By adding something to the start of the word - here it is 'DIS-' - the meaning has been changed so that it means 'the opposite of loyal'.

New beginnings

The posh name for the bit that is added to the front of the original (or 'root') word is a **'prefix'**. As well as the prefix *'dis-'*, there are other ones that make a word mean the opposite thing, such as *'im-'*, which changes *'possible'* into *'impossible'* and *'in-'* which can change *'formal'* to *'informal'*, for example.

Here are some other prefixes you may be familiar with: *'pre-'* as in *'preview'*, *'un-'* as in *'undo'* and *'unnecessary'*, *'re-'* as in *'replace'* and *'recover'* and *'mis-'* as in *'mistake'* and *'misplace'*.

Double trouble

Sometimes, when you add a prefix, it may mean that you find yourself with double letters in a word. This is because when adding prefixes, root words don't change. If it helps, you can remind yourself that root words are like the roots of trees: they stay put.

Using this rule, if you want to add the prefix *'un-'* to *'necessary'* it becomes *'unnecessary'*. Similarly, add *'im-'* to *'mature'* and you get *'immature'*. So as you can see, doubles are easy peasy!

Im possible

Perfect Endings

Adding letters to the end of a root word can also change its meaning. This is called a '**suffix**', such as '-*ed*', '-*ing*', '-*ly*', '-*ness*' and '-*less*'.

Some suffixes change the tense of the root word. '*I want a cake*' can be changed by adding '-*ed*': '*I wanted a cake*'.

This goes back to our section on tenses, on page 32. By adding '-*ed*' you can tell readers that you are talking in the past tense – perhaps you wanted cake but now the craving has passed or maybe you were lucky enough to get a slice. Yummy!

Suffixes can also change adjectives into adverbs – remember those from page 20? By adding '-*ly*' you can describe how someone does something: '*quickly*', '*quietly*', '*softly*'.

Keep or drop?

Unlike prefixes, root words do change for some suffixes. If the root word ends in a consonant and the suffix begins with one, all you need to do is stick them together: '*entertain*' becomes '*entertainment*', for example.

For words that end in 'e', drop the 'e' before adding a suffix: '*like*' becomes '*liked*' and '*joke*' becomes '*joking*'.

If the root word ends in a consonant followed by a 'y', change it to 'i': '*happy*' becomes '*happiness*'.

Short words ending in a consonant are doubled up: '*run*' becomes '*running*', '*hot*' becomes '*hotter*' and '*big*' becomes '*biggest*'.

You'll find a list of common prefixes and suffixes on page 95.

'I was at the beach yesterday. There were really big waves, crashing on the sand, and I saw a family setting up their picnic. Huge gusts of wind blew across the bay, so hard that it turned over their blue blanket. The two children were upset that it was too windy to have the picnic. I hear that the weather was much better here than it was on the coast.'

If you read the paragraph above aloud, you might notice something strange. The pairs of words in blue sound the same, but they are spelled differently and mean different things.

These are called '**homophones**'. If you want to be a homophone hero rather than having a huge headache on your hands, these examples will help you:

That's too bad!

It's easy to get 'to', 'too' and 'two' tangled. Here's how to sort them out:

'*Two*' is the easiest one to get sorted. It just means the number two, and you don't ever need to use it in any other way:

She bought two dresses in the sale.

'*To*' is a preposition (remember those from page 22?). So it can be used to say:

We went to town or *That book belongs to Sophie.*

'*Too*' is used for saying that there is 'too much' of something:
It was too hot to go cycling.

It is also used to mean 'as well':
We had a main course and a dessert, too.

There/their/they're!

It's very easy to tie yourself in knots over '*there*', '*their*' and '*they're*'.

Just remember to use '*there*' when you are talking about places: *the book belongs on the shelf over there.*

'*Their*' needs to be used when you are talking about something that belongs to more than one person: *their book collection is amazing!*

'*They're*' is only ever used to mean '*they are*': *they're meeting us at the theatre.*

Your or you're?

Confuse these two homophones and your teacher will gnash her teeth! Use '*your*' when you are talking about something that belongs to a person you are speaking to, so *your toothbrush* or *your house*. '*You're*' is short for 'you are', as in, *you're very good at spelling!*

of/off

This is another tricky pair. As a rule 'off' means 'not on', 'removed' or 'away from', so: *the light was off* and *he took off his coat*. On the other hand, 'of' is for things that belong to each other: *the bag of sweets*, for example.

Top Tip:

'Of' should never be used instead of 'have'. "*We could of won the game*" is a complete no-no!

Which witch is which?

A 'witch' is someone that casts spells, wears a pointy black hat and rides a broomstick. 'Which' is used to ask for more information about one or more things: *which top suits me best?* or to give extra information that may not be needed for the sentence to make sense: *the top, which I had bought on holiday last year, was perfect for the party.*

Wear/where

Which brings us neatly on to our next example. You '*wear*' clothes. '*Where*' tells you the location of something or someone: *where is she?*

Here/hear

When you listen, you '*hear*' things. '*Here*' is used to talk about the location of something, or when you are giving something to someone: *here you are.* The words '*here*' and '*there*' have matching spellings – they're both talking about locations.

Stationery/stationary

Don't get these muddled up. '*Stationery*' means pens, envelopes and rulers, which are often found in a desk. Helpfully, you'll find '*stationery*' at a '*stationers*' – not a '*stationars*'. Heavy traffic often leads to '*stationary*' cars, which means they are not moving.

Same but Different

As well as homophones, you also need to watch for other sneaky words that are spelled the same, but sound different. The posh word for these is a 'heteronym'. Try reading these examples aloud to really see the difference:

*Sarah will **present** (give) the **present** (gift) after the speeches.*

*The **minute** (precise moment) she saw the gift, Sarah was worried. It was **minute** (tiny).*

*The **wind** (weather) was blowing so hard that he knew it would be a struggle to **wind** (wrap up) the kite line.*

*My brother is teaching me **Polish** (a language) while I **polish** (clean) the silver.*

*I **produce** (make) knitted blankets and sell them with my home-grown **produce** (food).*

Confused? Well, don't panic. Most of the time, you can tell how to pronounce a word by looking at the words around it, which will give you the meaning. So, taking one of the examples above, which is talking about the wind 'blowing hard' – it's pretty easy to understand from this that the writer is talking about the weather. So, if you read a sentence with a heteronym in it, take some time to look at the words around it. You may need to read further sentences to be sure, but the clues should be there.

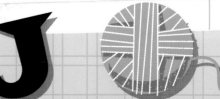

Let's look at some more:

*Be careful when you **close** (shut) the door. There's someone coming in **close** (near) behind you.*

*While they **rowed** (in a boat) on the river, they **rowed** (argued) loudly.*

*I got the **wound** (injury) when I **wound** up (coiled) the rusty cable.*

Getting the hang of them now? Thought so! Try these ones:

*She burst into **tears** (crying) when she saw the huge **tears** (rips) in her favourite dress.*

*Please don't **subject** me (make me do) to maths. It's my least favourite **subject** (topic).*

*You can **lead** (guide) a horse to water, but make sure it's not coming from **lead** (metal) pipes.*

*When she read the essay back, she was **content** (happy) with its **content** (what was in it).*

There are loads more heteronyms out there – far too many to list here. See how many others you can spot. You may be surprised by how many you know!

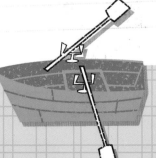

Decisions, Decisions!

So, as well as homophones, there are heteronyms to watch out for. But these aren't the only spelling curve balls the English language can throw to catch you unawares. There are also many other words that sound really alike, but are spelled slightly differently. Loads of people are tripped up by them - you might see these mistakes on the TV or even in newspapers. The good news is that we have some simple tricks so you know just what to do when you are served up with a spelling curve ball. So here are a few examples - CATCH!

Edition/addition

Have you seen the latest '*edition*' of your favourite magazine yet? Or have you bought the first '*edition*' of the next book in the series? Don't get this one confused with '*addition*'. That's what you do in maths. You can remember this one because 'addition' is used for 'adding' up numbers.

It's amazing what a difference one little letter can make, isn't it? How about this one – do you know the difference between ensure and insure?

Ensure/insure

When you '*ensure*', you are making sure something will happen. You '*insure*' a car or a house in case there is an incident. Make sure you pick the right one by remembering that 'insure' and 'incident' both start with an 'i'.

Loose/lose

If you '*lose*' something, you no longer have it, whereas '*loose*' means come free – the double letters in 'loose' and 'free' will help you remember this.

Compliment/complement

There's 'compliment', which means to give someone praise. Not to be confused with 'complement', which means something that adds something extra to make something better. So, you might *compliment* your friend on her outfit and tell her that it *complements* her blue eyes.

What about these words? They sound really similar but again they mean totally different things. Pick the wrong one and your readers may be very puzzled:

Access/excess

When you 'access' something you go in to a place or get hold of something. 'Excess' means too much – think of someone eating too many eggs.

Accept/except

'Accept' means to agree to something. 'Except' means not including. So you might say: "I will accept all the cakes, except for the mouldy one."

Bought/brought

Goods are 'bought' at the shops, when you have remembered to bring something you have 'brought' it with you. Another way of remembering it is: 'buy' – 'bought', 'bring' – 'brought'.

Through/thorough

You go 'through' a doorway, but if you check something really carefully, you are being 'thorough'.

Shhh! Silent Letters

Just when you think you've nailed this spelling business, BAM! You are taken by surprise by the ninjas of the word world: silent letters. Just like ninja warriors, they are there, but you don't always realise until it's too late! Don't get caught out - follow these rules and you will spot these letter ninjas before they get the better of you...

Knock-kneed knights and knives

Knives are dangerous, not only in the real world but also in the word world, because they contain the dreaded silent 'k' in the 'kn' sound. Just like 'knock', 'knee' and 'knight'. Now you are in the 'know', you can make sure that 'kn' doesn't slash your spelling score!

Gnomes gnashing gnats

Gnomes gnash gnats quietly – they never say their 'g'. Now you know this, it's a 'sign' that you're becoming a letter master!

Dumb combs

There's the silent 'b' in words ending 'mb', such as 'comb', 'dumb' 'limb' and 'bomb'. The 'b' is also silent in 'doubt' and 'debt'.

The edge of a bridge

The 'd' stays silent in the fridge, on a ledge and a hedge, when you wear a badge or dodge the edge.

Whistling castles

'T's' stay silent in 'castles' and when people 'whistle' or 'rustle'. Remind yourself about this letter ninja by thinking about people sitting in a castle, drinking tea in silence!

No 'L'

'L' 'should' be silent when you 'talk' and when you feel 'calm'.

Guardian guinea pigs and guitars

The 'u' is silent for 'guardian', 'guinea pigs' and 'guitars', as well as 'biscuit' and 'guide'.

Dropped aitches

'Chemists', 'whales' and 'ghosts' don't say their 'h', 'whatever' the occasion.

W wrapped whole

'W' stays under 'wraps' when you say it – don't forget it when you 'write' it down.

Silent arguments

Watch out for silent 'ue' sounds at the end words such as 'plague', 'catalogue', 'league' and 'tongue'. Don't get caught out by 'argue' as the 'ue' isn't silent – argue disagrees with the rule.

Hard to hear

Then there are the letters that are not quite silent, but are hard to hear. Watch out for words such as 'difference', 'library', 'business'. Not to mention 'interesting', 'jewellery' and 'family'. If ever you get stuck on your not-quite-silent letters, try saying the word out loud in slow motion to uncover any lurking quiet ones. If you're still not sure, you'll have to resort to the ultimate defence in the battle against letter ninjas – a dictionary!

Really Tricky Words

You've sorted the silent words and those that are hard to hear, but what about the real troublemakers? How on earth do you remember the really rotten words? Here are some of the toughest words to spell, that often trip people up. You'll find some handy hints next to each one to help you build up your spelling strength and remember how to handle the humdingers!

acceptable – **accept** that you are **able** at spelling.

accidentally – don't get tripped up by this one! Remember how to spell the **'-ally'** ending by learning: **all** accidents make you **y**ell.

accommodate – think of a hotel room with the number 22 for the two 'c's' and two 'm's' in this word.

address – when you write a letter you **add** the name to the envelope then **s**tick on a **s**tamp – this will help you remember the double letters.

attendance – to remember the second 'a', think of it as going to a **da**nce.

Antarctic – think of an **ant** in the **Arctic**, to help you learn this one.

beautiful – you can remember the tricky spelling at the start by learning: **B**eing **E**xtra **A**ttractive **U**nless **T**ired.

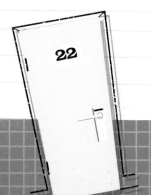

believe – you can get the 'i' and 'e' in the right order by remembering that there's a **lie** in believe.

breath/breathe – breath is a noun, so use breath when you are talking about *'bad breath'* or *'taking a breath'*. 'Breathe' is a verb: something you do when you breathe in and out. You can remember to add the 'e' if you think about breathing out being **e**xhaling.

calendar – a calen**dar** shows when **da**tes **are**.

committee – have **m**any **m**eetings with **t**wo **t**ea breaks.

definite – to fin**i**sh this word, you need two 'i's'.

disappear – remember that one **s**pell can make **p**retty **p**owerful magic to remember that you need one 's' and two 'p's'.

eight – this sentence will tell you exactly how to spell 'eight':
'**E**ven **I**cebergs **G**et **H**ot **T**onight'.

embarrassed – when people are embarrassed they go **r**eally **r**ed because they feel **s**o **s**illy.

exaggerate – **EX**ercise **A**nd **G**ood **G**rub **E**nergize **R**unners **A**nd **T**eachers **E**qually.

familiar – If you remember *'my family is familiar, so I-Always-Recognize them'* it will help you remember the 'I-A-R' ending.

forty – we have forty helpers, so we don't need you (U).

government – **govern men t**oday.

grammar – A+ pupils remember it has two A's!

guarantee – **G**rumpy **U**ntil **A RANT E**xplains **E**verything.

immediately – **media t**ells **e**veryone immediately.

library – it's **rar**e to find lions in a library.

lightning – remember the unusual '-ning' ending by learning *'lightning is exciting but it doesn't have an e'.*

mischievous – lots of people pronounce this wrong, which makes them spell it incorrectly. It should be said: 'MIS-CHI-VUS' - this will help you to remember that there's no 'i' in the bit at the end.

necessary – one 'c' and two 's's' are 'necessary'.

occasion – think of it being a birthday, with: **C**ake, **C**andles and **S**inging to help you remember the two 'c's' and one 's'.

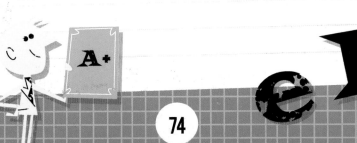

parallel – it's easy to get this one wrong and miss off the second 'l', so just think of the two 'l's' in the middle as being like train tracks that run through the middle of the word.

privilege – remember that the middle of this word is tricky, in fact it's **'vile'**!

probably – **P**upils **R**eally **O**vereat **B**iscuits **A**nd **B**ananas **L**oudly. **Y**um!

rhythm – **R**eally **H**appy **Y**aks **T**ackle **H**orror **M**ovies

separate – an 'r' sits between two 'a's', keeping them sep**ara**te.

surprise – **S**eeing **U**nicorns **R**acing **P**andas **R**esults **I**n **S**urprised **E**xpressions.

Wednesday – the easiest way to remember this as 'Wed-NES-day'

Top Tip:

Many people find there are a few words they get stuck on when they try to spell them. You've heard this a few times, but if in doubt, get a dictionary out. There's no harm in checking, just to be sure!

Chapter 5

Super-Advanced Stuff

Hopefully by now you are a grammar guru with perfect punctuation skills. However, things don't stop here. When you are writing and speaking, there are some other important points that will help you to polish your prose.

Handle with care

Do you remember the example *'Let's eat Grandma!'* from page 44? It showed how something as simple as a missing comma can result in all sorts of confusion. But that's not all. When you are writing, you also need to make sure you use the right words, or you will change the meaning completely.

To help you with your writing, you need to remember the four 'c's: CHOOSE with CARE to ensure you are CLEAR and CONCISE. Then your audience will know exactly what you mean.

But picking the right words isn't just limited to meaning. You can also select words to add atmosphere and feeling, which will magically bring your language to life. It can be the difference between a piece of straightforward, quite dull text and something that really draws your reader in and makes them want to know more.

Read on to find out how to become a true word wizard.

Spice it Up!

When you are cooking a meal, adding some extra ingredients can make a bland menu come to life. The same is true of writing and, as with cooking, you should never be afraid to experiment. Adding a splash of something different can produce surprising results - you may find you have created a masterpiece, or it might be a bit of a mess, but having the confidence to try different combinations is the key.

When you are writing, you can really give your text some pizzazz by using metaphors and similes. There's more on these below and on pages 80–81. But beware, some metaphors and similes are used so often that they have become clichés – boring or overused phrases that don't add anything to your writing. It's the English equivalent of still liking last year's boy band – we're sick of the sight of them and we've all moved on, thank you very much!

My sister is a witch!

In the sentence above, your sister has been described as being a witch. She probably isn't – unless she wears a pointy hat, rides a broomstick and has a black cat – but you are describing her this way for effect, possibly because she won't let you borrow her new phone to play on. The posh word for this is a **'metaphor'**.

Metaphors are used all the time, such as: *'she's a star'*, *'my brother is a pain in the neck'* and *'life is a roller coaster'* for example.

Metaphoric mash-ups

Metaphors are often misused. The most common problem is when people mash them together so they don't make sense at all:

'We'll burn that bridge when we cross it' is a good example. This is a mix of two metaphors: the first is *'we'll cross that bridge when we come to it'*, which means you will deal with something that may happen when it comes up. The second is *'don't burn your bridges'*, which means always leave yourself a way to go back to something. For example, if you decided to quit the football team, your mum might say, *"don't burn your bridges"*, which means be nice to your coach, even though you are leaving, because you want to be able to go back if you change your mind.

Mixed metaphors can leave your readers feeling like their brain has been frazzled, rather than helping them enjoy your super-duper writing skills. Here's another mixed-metaphor-mash-up to avoid: *'to make an omelette, don't crack all the eggs in one basket.'* Ouch!

If you use them creatively, metaphors can really spice up your writing. They can add drama and atmosphere to a story and there's no limit to how inventive you can be with them. How about these examples:

The wind whispered around them.
The night sky was black velvet.

But remember to avoid clichés such as *'it was the icing on the cake'* and *'so quiet you could hear a pin drop'*, unless you want to bore your readers to tears!

Cool as a Cucumber

Have you ever watched a film and heard a character use a cheesy chat-up line such as 'your eyes are like stars sparkling in the sky...'?

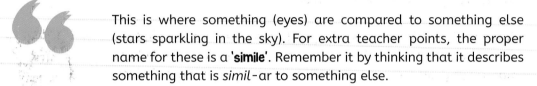

This is where something (eyes) are compared to something else (stars sparkling in the sky). For extra teacher points, the proper name for these is a **'simile'**. Remember it by thinking that it describes something that is *simil*-ar to something else.

Similes use connectives such as *'like'* or *'as'*. For example, *'he was as bold as brass'* and *'the meat was as tough as old boots'* or *'they fought like cat and dog'*. Similes often paint vivid pictures for readers, such as this famous quote from the poet W. H. Auden: *'my face looks like a wedding cake left out in the rain.'*

It's quite common, when you are out and about, to hear people saying, *'She was, like, so angry with me!'* or *'He was, like, so gorgeous!'.* They may contain 'like' but these are not similes, they are examples of poor English so keep them out of your writing!

That's so last week! (Clichés)

As with metaphors, many similes are overused. Be careful when you use them or you run the risk of sounding as cheesy as the chat-up line above. Try to come up with your own images instead and, if

something sounds very familiar, avoid it unless you want to sound really dated! This example is cobbled together from some well-known phrases that people wheel out all too often:

At the end of the day, when it comes down to it, I'll get straight to the point and stop beating about the bush.

If it helps, think of clichés as being a little like wearing clothes that are two years out of fashion on your non-uniform day. OMG! How embarrassing! Just as you would do anything to avoid a fashion nightmare, make sure that you are aware of clichés when you write and try not to use them if you can.

Clichés are often quite long-winded, too. If you look at something you've written, you'll probably find you can lose a few words and make your writing snappier. So for example you might change the cliché *'in this day and age'* to *'today'*.

Here are a few clunky clichés to keep out of your writing at all costs:

When all is said and done
To get to the point
At the end of the day
White as snow
Black as night
The fact of the matter is
To be honest
Needless to say
Before I knew it

Watch Out For Word Traps

'Basically, I'm literally dying, actually!' Ummm... no, you're not. Unless you are feeling like a spell in A&E may be necessary, in which case you should stop reading and call an ambulance.

The above is an example of words such as *'literally'*, *'basically'*, *'actually'* slapped into sentences where they are not needed, making teachers literally cringe.

This is a good spot to remind you of the 'time and place rule.' If you want to use these phrases when you are chatting informally with your friends, that's no problem. Speaking with a formal hat on though, the way in which these words are used isn't correct. So it's best to keep them out of schoolwork and other formal situations, 'basically.'

More tricky traps

There are many other word traps to watch out for. A lot of people commonly use *'of'* instead of *'have'* when they write or speak. *'I could have passed with top marks if I hadn't missed the exam'* is fine. *'I could of gone to university if I had taken the exam'* will not impress anyone.

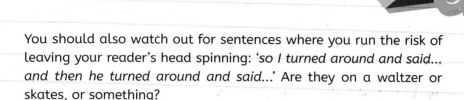

You should also watch out for sentences where you run the risk of leaving your reader's head spinning: *'so I turned around and said... and then he turned around and said...'* Are they on a waltzer or skates, or something?

Another no-no is using words such as *'goes'* or *'went'* when you are talking about a conversation or event when there was no movement involved at all: *then he goes, "No way!" and I went, "Yeah, it's true!".* Again, know your situation – this is fine when you are hanging about with your mates but steer clear for formal situations.

What about txt spk?

Everyone knows that in texts or on social media, when you say *OMG!* you are expressing surprise, or if you *LOL!* you are laughing. So why can't you use it in your schoolwork? The simple answer again is that it's fine for informal situations, but shouldn't be used for more formal situations, such as your schoolwork, letter writing or in the workplace.

Getting emotional

The same is true of 'emoticons' - the signs used online to express your emotions. They help people to know when you are joking ;-) :-P or when you are shocked :-O but if you use them in an English essay, your teacher is likely to look like this :-/. So remember, emoticons are fine and dandy for informal online chatting or texts, but steer well clear in your school work or a letter to your Auntie Joan.

If you've forgotten to do your homework and you're in your teacher's bad books, here are some big words to chuck into the conversation. With any luck they'll be dazzled by your brilliance and will forget all about the homework! These ideas are perfect for sprinkling in your creative writing.

All the a's alliterate

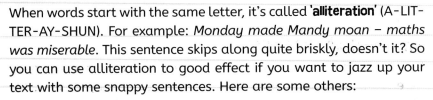

When words start with the same letter, it's called **'alliteration'** (A-LIT-TER-AY-SHUN). For example: *Monday made Mandy moan – maths was miserable*. This sentence skips along quite briskly, doesn't it? So you can use alliteration to good effect if you want to jazz up your text with some snappy sentences. Here are some others:

Claire craved cream cakes constantly.
Perfectly polished prose (did you spot that one on page 27?).

Exaggeration station

I was chased by a bee yesterday, it was the size of a T-rex! Chances are that the bee was probably no bigger than a thumbnail. But people can use obvious exaggeration like this to make others laugh. It can be really effective if you're telling a story, but don't overuse it or people will call you a drama llama! For extra teacher brownie points, this is called **'hyperbole'** (HY-PER-BO-LEE).

Sounds like...

The computer mouse went click! The cat miaowed. She slurped her drink. These phrases all use something called **'onomatopoeia'** (ON-O-MAT-O-PEA-AH) – which means that they imitate the sound they make. *'Plop!'*, *'Splat!'*, *'Boing!'* and *'Crash!'* are further examples. They can really bring your writing to life – think of them as being like the sound effects in a film, helping the audience to experience the story with all their senses. But a word of warning. Choose them with care and don't use too many of them, otherwise your readers may get distracted by all the noise!

Don't make me say it twice!

Sometimes, if you put two words together, you'll find that one of them is not needed, because it says the same thing twice. The best example of this is 'free gift'. You can lose either word, as something that is free is a gift and a gift is always free. This is called **'tautology'** (TOR-TOLO-GEE).

The opposite problem

If a phrase contains two words that sit next to each other and mean different or opposite things, that is known as an **'oxymoron'** (OXY-MOR-ON). One example would be *'awfully good'*. Other examples include *'almost exactly'*, *'a definite maybe'* and *'only choice'*. You can use them when you write as a witty line to make readers laugh, to point out a silly situation or even for dramatic effect to make readers pause and think about something.

Perfect paradoxes

A **'paradox'** contains two statements that can be true, but not at the same time. So the statement contradicts itself. *'to be cruel to be kind'* is a paradox, as you can't be cruel and kind at the same time. Another example is *'deep down you are really shallow'*. A paradox is useful if you want to make your readers look more closely at the meaning of your words. At first, a sentence may seem straightforward, but when a reader really thinks about it, they may find that there is a deeper meaning. Take for example the sentence: *'I am a compulsive liar'*. At first glance, you may think that this means a person is a liar, but if you pause and think about it again, you might find yourself wondering whether they are telling the truth about being a liar...

The Right Writing Style

When you are set a writing task, it's important to make sure that you choose a writing style that suits the job:

Red-hot reports

Reports need to be factual and to the point. They are useful for writing up science experiments, for example. You must back up findings with evidence and possibly diagrams. No using metaphors and similes here!

Roaring recounts

A recount is written in the past tense and may be used to tell people about something that has happened to you, such as what you did in the summer holidays. It is factual, but you can also have fun, depending on the topic. If you are talking about your summer holidays, you could use metaphors or similes to describe the experiences you had. You might also include facts and figures about the place you visited.

Excellent essays

Often, students are asked to write an essay arguing for or against a topic. An essay usually starts with one or two sentences to introduce the topic, followed by different ideas or facts about it, with details to support your ideas. A final paragraph summarizes the writer's findings, or ideas for the reader to take away from the subject. A good essay requires preparation – you may need to look up facts and figures to support your ideas. Plan out the main points of your essay and how you will wrap it up.

Brilliant book reviews

At school, you may be asked to write a book review. This should be factual and is usually written in the past tense. Start with the title and author of the book, followed by a brief summary of the plot – make sure you don't give everything away! You can then outline what you liked and disliked about it, with some examples to support your thoughts, followed by an overall verdict – did you like it and would you recommend it to other readers?

Perfect poetry

Poetry is the perfect chance for you to get creative. You can bring in a bit of everything – alliteration, onomatopoeia, metaphors, similes, to name but a few! Experiment with the words you choose to change the pace and feeling of your work – the possibilities are endless!

Super stories

You also have more freedom to choose your words if you are writing a story, but your tale still needs a beginning, middle and ending. Your writing needs a good structure, characters and setting, as well as a plot that keeps your readers hooked. A strong opening line will grab the reader's attention, such as this from Terry Pratchett in his book *Johnny and the Dead*: '*Johnny never knew for certain why he started seeing the dead.*' It stops you in your tracks momentarily, but urges you to read on.

Top Tip:

When you are writing, pop it all down on paper, leave it for a while, then go back and polish it up. Take out wordy bits, watch out for the clichés and be sure everything is clear. It often helps to read it aloud. Do the words flow smoothly? If they don't and a word needs changing, a thesaurus can help you to find other words with the same meaning.

Letters and Formal Emails

Knowing how to be a letter-writing legend and epic at emailing is always useful. You'll need it for all sorts of things, such as saying thank you for your Christmas presents, writing fan mail to your favourite celebs, or applying for a job.

Lovely letters

Start by writing your address top right. Leave a line space after your address, then add the date underneath. Below this, put the name and address of the person you are writing to on the left.

> 141 My Street
> My Town
> My County
> PO5 7ME
>
> day/month/year

The Manager
My Dream Job Limited
Gold Street
Richville
IN4 7OB

Leave a line, then underneath their address, you start the letter. If you don't know the person's name, or whether they are male or female you should write:

Dear Sir/Madam,

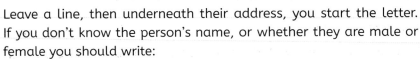

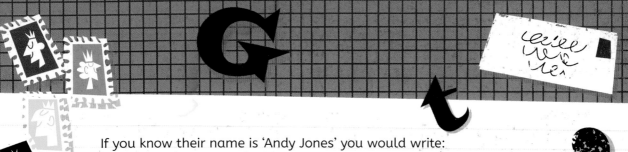

If you know their name is 'Andy Jones' you would write:

Dear Mr Jones,

Make sure that you organize your letter into clear paragraphs. The first should explain why you are writing. Once you have included all the information you need to put down, you can wrap it up by saying something about what you hope will happen next such as: *'I look forward to hearing from you.'*

Then it's time to sign off. For friends and family it would be fine to write *'love'* or *'from'*, but you can't use those in a formal letter. To work out how to sign off, go back to the *'Dear...'* line. If you have used *'Sir'*, *'Madam'* or *'Sir/Madam'* you sign off with:

Yours faithfully,
Your name

If you have addressed the person by name: *'Dear Amy Smith'*, you sign off with:

Yours sincerely,
Your name

If you find it hard to remember whether to use sincerely or faithfully, remember: *'Sir and sincerely should never be seen.'*

Excellent emails

You can use a similar format for formal emails, leaving out the addresses and dates. Sign-offs tend to be slightly less formal. For example, sometimes people use *'Kind regards'* or *'Best wishes'*. If you're not sure what to use and you don't know the person you are writing to, stick with *'Yours faithfully'* or *'Yours sincerely'*.

And, Finally...

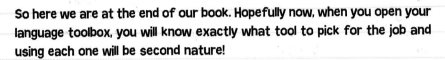

So here we are at the end of our book. Hopefully now, when you open your language toolbox, you will know exactly what tool to pick for the job and using each one will be second nature!

Whatever you do though, remember that although there are rules to the English language, this is only half the story. The words that you choose and the way that you put them together is up to you. Some rules are there to be broken and it is only by experimenting with words that we find new ways of expressing ourselves.

Another important point to make is that knowing what to do doesn't change YOU. It's just a useful piece of kit that you can rely on so you know what to do when a formal situation zips up unexpectedly. Dashing off a thank-you letter to Great Auntie Joan? Simple! Writing to apply for your dream job? No sweat! Conjuring up the novel that will earn you a fortune? Consider it done! Greeting Her Maj without majorly embarrassing your mum? No worries! Just pop on your formal hat, crack open the toolbox and wow people with your amazing language skills – it's easy peasy when you know how!

Examples of irregular verbs:

verb	Past	Present	Future
be	I was	I am	I will be
go	I went	I go	I will go
do	I did	I do	I will do
begin	I began	I begin	I will begin
buy	I bought	I buy	I will buy
catch	I caught	I catch	I will catch
drive	I drove	I drive	I will drive
eat	I ate	I eat	I will eat
find	I found	I find	I will find
get	I got	I get	I will get
give	I gave	I give	I will give
have	I had	I have	I will have
hide	I hid	I hide	I will hide
keep	I kept	I keep	I will keep
know	I knew	I know	I will know
lay	I lay	I lie	I will lie
leave	I left	I leave	I will leave
make	I made	I make	I will make
mean	I met	I meet	I will meet
ride	I rode	I ride	I will ride
ring	I rang	I ring	I will ring
run	I ran	I run	I will run
say	I said	I say	I will say
see	I saw	I see	I will see
sell	I sold	I sell	I will sell
sleep	I slept	I sleep	I will sleep
shake	I shook	I shake	I will shake
speak	I spoke	I speak	I will speak
swim	I swam	I swim	I will swim
take	I took	I take	I will take
tell	I told	I tell	I will tell
throw	I threw	I throw	I will throw
win	I won	I win	I will win
write	I wrote	I write	I will write

Glossary
(Fancy words to you and me)

adjective - words that add description such as 'tall' or 'dirty'.

adverb - a word that tells you how something is done, such as 'happily' or 'quickly'.

alliteration - words next to or close to each other that begin with the same letter. 'Big blue ball', for example.

apostrophe - either used to show where letters have been left out ('don't', 'can't', 'it'll', for example) or to show something belongs ('Lucy's pen', for example).

cliché - an idea or phrase that is very over-used.

connective - a joining word, such as 'and', 'or', 'but', 'so'.

heteronym - a word that is spelled the same way, but has different meanings depending on how it is pronounced. 'Present' can mean 'gift' or 'being there', for example.

homophones - two words that sound the same but are spelled differently and mean different things. 'Blue' and 'blew', for example.

hyperbole - over-exaggeration, often used for effect. Such as, 'It's taken me a million years to do my maths homework'.

metaphor - describes something as being something else. 'She was a dragon', for example.

noun - a naming word. Proper nouns are the name of a particular person or place, such as 'Amelia' or 'Canada', common nouns are things that you can put 'the', 'a' or 'an' in front of, such as 'a book'. Collective nouns are names for groups of people or things, such as 'class', for example.

object - the thing that the action of a sentence is being done to.

onomatopoeia - a word that imitates the sound it makes.

oxymoron - a phrase where there are two words together that mean different, or opposite things, such as *'seriously funny'*.

paradox - a phrase that contains two statements that can be true, but not at the same time such as *'save money by spending it'*.

prefix - something added to the beginning of a word to change its meaning, such as adding *'dis-'* before *'honest'* to make *'dishonest'*.

preposition - position words that tell you how, when, or where something happened, such as *'on'*, *'in'* or *'behind'*, for example.

plural - a word ending that tells you there is more than one, such as *'books'* or *'matches'*.

pronoun - a word used instead of a noun that has already been mentioned, such as *'I'*, *'you'*, *'we'* and *'they'*.

simile - a phrase where one thing is compared to another such as, *'he was like a bear with a sore head'*.

subject - the person or thing that is doing an action.

suffix - something added to the end of a word to change it, such as adding *'-less'* to *'meaning'* to make *'meaningless'*.

tense - past, present or future form of a verb that tells you if something has happened, is happening or is yet to happen.

verb - an action or *'doing'* word, such as *'run'*, *'bake'*, *'sleep'* or *'fly'*.

Adjectives

Huge, tiny, fast, small, big, pretty, ugly, good, bad, heavy, sweet

Adverbs:

'How' words:

brilliantly, quickly, quietly, softly, silently, magnificently, happily, easily

'When' words:

soon, immediately, today, now, yesterday, already, before

'Where' words:

in, out, above, behind, here, everywhere, nowhere

'How much' words:

almost, quite, completely, very, so, too, less, hardly

Auxiliary (helping) verbs:

am/was/is/are/were/been/being/be

have/had/has

do/does/did

can/could

may/might

shall/should

will/would

must

ought to

used to

Comparatives

faster, smaller, bigger, tinier, prettier, uglier, heavier, sweeter

Superlatives

fastest, smallest, biggest, tiniest, prettiest, ugliest, heaviest, sweetest

Connectives

above all, afterwards, also, alternatively, as already stated, as a result, as well as, consequently, despite this, especially, eventually, finally, firstly, for example, furthermore, however, in addition, in conclusion, indeed, in particular, later, likewise, meanwhile, moreover, nevertheless, next, notably, on the contrary, on the other hand, otherwise, secondly, significantly, similarly, then, therefore, thirdly, to summarize

Conjunctions

although, and, after, apart from, as long as, because, before, as, but, even if, even though, if, or, provided that, since, so, so that, unless, until, when, whereas, whenever, whether or not, while, whilst

Coordinating conjunctions

and, as, because, but, for, nor, or, so, yet

Subordinate conjunctions

after, although, as, as soon as, because, before, by the time, even if, even though, every time, if, in case, just in case, now that, once, only if, since, though, unless, until, when, whenever, whereas, whether or not, while

Prefixes (examples in brackets)

anti- (anticlockwise), bi- (biannual), de- (decrease), em- (empower), ex- (exhale), il- (illegal), im- (impossible), in- (invisible), mis- (misplace), non- (nonsense), re- (reappear), un- (unusual), pre- (prehistoric)

Suffixes (examples in brackets)

-able (comfortable), -al (comical), -er (richer), -est (biggest), -ful (beautiful), -ily (happily), -ible (terrible), -ing (dancing), -less (speechless), -ly (truly), -ness (happiness), -y (messy)